DRUGS AND POLITICS

The war against drugs is worldwide.

DRUGS AND POLITICS

Peggy Santamaria

THE ROSEN PUBLISHING GROUP, INC.
NEW YORK

Published in 1994 by The Rosen Publishing Group, Inc.
29 East 21st Street, New York, NY 10010

First Edition

Library of Congress Cataloging-in-Publication Data

Santamaria, Peggy.
    Drugs and politics / Peggy Santamaria. — 1st ed.
        p.   cm. — (The Drug abuse prevention library)
    Includes bibliographical references and index.
    ISBN 0-8239-1703-7
    1. Drug abuse—Government policy—Juvenile literature.
    2. Narcotics, Control of—Government policy—Juvenile literature.
    3. Narcotics and crime—Juvenile literature.
    [1. Drug abuse.   2. Narcotics, Control of.]
    I. Title. II. Series.
HV5809.5.S26   1994
363.4'5'0973—dc20   94-1024
                                                        CIP
                                                        AC

Manufactured in the United States of America

Contents

Stories involving drugs make the news almost every day.

CHAPTER 1

The Need For Education

Almost every day we can turn on television and see a story related to drug abuse. On the news we see the violence of killing over drugs. It may be rival gangs fighting over turf. Often, we see innocent bystanders caught in the cross-fire and killed. Sometimes the bystander is a small child.

On live action shows we see police doing their job busting drug dealers. Large amounts of money are involved. So are deadly assault weapons.

The problems and the violence caused by drug abuse are not just on television. We can turn off television just by pushing a button, but the drug problem will still be there.

8 It is part of our daily lives. We can't just turn it off or turn away from it.

The Harm to Us All

Drugs hurt us all. They can hurt us as individuals. They can hurt members of our families. They hurt the communities we live in. They hurt the peoples of the United States and many other countries.

How do drugs hurt us? What can we do to protect ourselves? Education about drugs is a big part of the answer to those questions. Learning about drugs and the problems they create is an important first step in solving the problem.

Before we try to fix anything, we need to know how it is broken. To make something right, we need to know what is wrong with it. A doctor does not begin surgery without examining the patient. A mechanic does not take apart a car engine before finding out what is wrong with it.

We, too, need knowledge about the enormous problem of drug abuse before we can help fix it.

U.S. Efforts

In the United States during the 1980s, lawmakers responded to the public outcry

Drug use among teens has decreased in recent years.

10 to stop drug abuse and the violence and crime associated with it. The Office for Substance Abuse Prevention (OSAP) was created in the Department of Health and Human Services. This office helped get money for programs in schools and colleges to teach about drug abuse.

In 1988 the Office of National Drug Abuse Policy was established. Its purpose is to coordinate and oversee the various drug prevention programs installed by the government.

Many parents and citizens also began setting up programs. They formed community groups to teach young people about the problems of drug abuse. They began working through the schools and the community centers to reach children. They went to the politicians and the school officials to ask for help.

Promising Results

As these education programs developed, the use of drugs by teens began to decrease. In 1979 more high school seniors were using drugs than ever before in history. By 1991 the use of drugs by high school seniors had gone down by 58 percent. Also by 1991 the number of people using cocaine had dropped by 1 million,

and the number of people using marijuana had dropped by nearly 2 million.

The politicians and the people see this
as both good news and bad news. The
bad news is that far too many people are
still abusing drugs. The good news is that
the programs are beginning to work. The
challenge to the politicians and people
running the programs is to find ways to
make the programs even more effective.
They know that millions more people
need to be reached.

Because there is still much to do, the
government drug prevention efforts continue. The programs have three parts:

1. Education to make people stop
   using drugs
2. Law enforcement to protect people
   from drug-related crimes
3. Treatment for those addicted to
   drugs.

All three parts must work effectively if
there is to be change.

CHAPTER 2

Where Drugs Come From: The World Picture

*T*he streets and the schools of big cities and small towns across the United States are full of illegal drugs. Where do these drugs come from and who produces them? Let's look at the examples of marijuana, cocaine, and heroin. All three of these drugs start out as crops in a field. Each crop goes through various phases of processing before it ends up on the street for sale as a drug.

The steps involved in producing illegal drugs are like the process of making a loaf of bread. The farmer grows the wheat and sells it to the mill to be refined into flour. The flour is then sold to a bakery, where it is made into bread for sale to wholesalers. These middlemen then ship

There are many steps in the production of the illegal drugs people buy on the streets.

the bread to stores, where it is bought by consumers.

So it is with the production of illegal drugs. Many steps are involved, and the drugs come from many countries.

Marijuana

The marijuana that is sold in the United States comes mainly from producers in the United States, Mexico, Jamaica, Colombia, and Thailand.

Marijuana is grown illegally in various parts of the United States. The crops are sold to wholesalers, who buy in very large quantities. Because the wholesaler buys so

14 | much, he or she gets a lower price. The wholesaler sells the drug to retailers, called dealers. The dealers then sell the marijuana to customers on streets all over the country.

Mexico

Some marijuana sold in the United States comes from Mexico. Mexico shares borders with Texas, New Mexico, Arizona, and California. The marijuana is grown in rural areas and shipped to points along those state borders. It is smuggled across the border and sold to the wholesalers in the U.S. Crossing the border is risky and difficult. Those who smuggle the drug charge a high price. The wholesalers then sell it to dealers across the country.

Jamaica

An island in the Caribbean Sea, Jamaica is about 500 miles southeast of the United States. The Jamaican farmers sell their marijuana to brokers. The brokers have the drug smuggled into the U.S., usually by boat or plane. This is dangerous business. Once the marijuana is in the U.S., the brokers sell it to wholesalers, who distribute it to dealers in cities and small towns.

Colombia

Yet another source of marijuana sold in the U.S. is Colombia, a country in northwestern South America. The marijuana grown in Colombia has a longer route to the States, but the steps involved in its journey from farm to city street are the same. Many hands and millions of dollars are involved from the grower to the wholesaler to the dealer.

Thailand

Marijuana also comes to the U.S. from Asia, on the other side of the world. In any direction from Thailand, foreign borders and oceans must be crossed to get to the U.S. From the growers in Thailand, the marijuana is sold to the brokers, who arrange to sell it to U.S. wholesalers for distribution to local dealers. And everyone involved charges money for service.

Cocaine

Cocaine comes to the U.S. from three main sources: Bolivia, Colombia, and Peru. On a map you can see the relative locations of these three South American countries. Colombia is the farthest north; Peru lies south of Colombia, and Bolivia is southeast of Peru.

Dealers sell cocaine to customers on streets all over
the United States.

Cocaine is made from leaves of the
coca plant. More steps are required to
produce cocaine than marijuana. So its
journey from the field of the grower to
the street dealer is even longer.

Processing the Drug

In Bolivia and Peru the coca leaves are
harvested by farmers and sold to people
who make them into coca paste. The
paste is then sold again and made into
cocaine base. In a third step, the base is
sold to be made into cocaine HCL (cocaine hydrochloride). In this form the
drug is smuggled to the United States,
usually through Florida. Wholesalers buy
the cocaine HCL and dilute it. They add
other chemicals to make it weaker, so
they have more to sell. The wholesalers
then sell it to the dealers, who dilute it
again before selling it on the streets.

In Colombia the process is different.
The coca leaves are smuggled in from
another country to be processed into
cocaine. Large organizations called cartels
control the drug production and trafficking. One powerful cartel in Colombia is
in the city of Cali. These cartels employ
many people and have great influence
because of their wealth and strength.

18 | *Heroin*

Heroin comes into the U.S. from three major areas: Mexico, Southwest Asia, and Southeast Asia.

Heroin is derived from the crop of opium poppies. In Mexico, large organizations control the growing of the poppies and the refining of the plants into opium and heroin. They also arrange for the smuggling of the heroin into the U.S. By the time the heroin reaches the U.S. wholesalers, it has been diluted. The wholesalers will dilute it once more before selling it to the dealers.

Southwest Asia

Pakistan, Afghanistan, and Iran are three countries clustered together in Southwest Asia. These countries cooperate in the processing, refining, and distribution of heroin. Several countries in the Middle East also participate in the business. The opium poppies are grown and harvested in Pakistan and Afghanistan. The opium is then sold to laboratories to be made into morphine base and then into heroin. It is smuggled through many countries, changing hands and being diluted many times. By the time the heroin reaches the

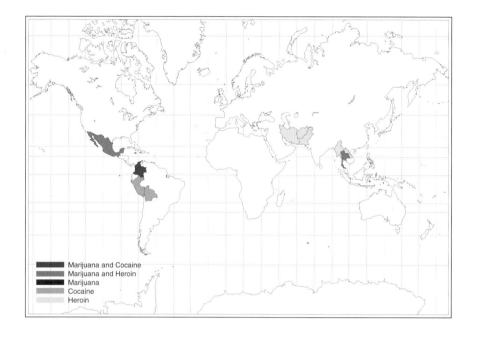

Marijuana and Cocaine
Marijuana and Heroin
Marijuana
Cocaine
Heroin

U.S., the price has gone up many times and the purity has gone down.

Southeast Asia

Burma, Laos, and Thailand are major sources of heroin. These Southeast Asian countries are called the "Golden Triangle" because of their heavy production of the drug. Burma is the major grower of the opium poppy. The opium, morphine, and heroin are made in laboratories in the hills of the Golden Triangle. From there the heroin begins its long journey to the U.S.

CHAPTER 3

Economics and Politics of Drug Production

*A*s we have seen, the major countries that produce drugs are far-flung. Their peoples speak different languages, have different customs, and follow different religions. Nevertheless, some similarities link them together.

For one thing, all these countries have economic problems. Economics refers to the wealth of a country and how it is shared by the people and used by the government. The wealth can be in the form of money earned or in natural resources such as gold, silver, or good farmland. The economic situation of a country may be judged by whether or not the people have the necessities of life such as food, shelter, and medical services.

Education and transportation may also be | *21*
considered in the economic picture.

Another similarity among the drug-producing countries is that they have had political problems. In some cases, these problems have been violent and long-lasting.

Mexico

Mexico is not poor compared to many other countries. It has schools, medical facilities, and modern cities. It manufactures products and raises crops that are used in Mexico and exported to other countries for sale.

Many Mexicans live well in the big cities, but many more live in poverty. The poor live on the rural hillsides and crowd into the rundown parts of the cities, where they cannot find work.

Problems of Reform

Many of the presidents of Mexico have worked for social reform. They have tried to improve the living conditions of the poor. But the government has been deeply in debt for many years. There is not enough money to provide all the rural areas with food and medical care.

With the rise in drug use in the U.S. in the 1970s, the Mexican farmers found

Pablo Escobar, former head of the Medellín drug cartel,
was killed in 1993.

that by raising marijuana they could earn enough to feed their families.

The Mexican government opposes the illegal drug production. It cooperates with the U.S. to fight the drug trade. But the government does not have the resources to pay for the law-enforcement and social programs that would be necessary to replace the illegal production of drugs.

Colombia

Colombia is a land of mountains, valleys, plains, and jungles. About 80 percent of the people live in the Andes Mountains. Cities like Bogotá, the capital, have large modern buildings. There is wealth in Colombia, but it is not evenly distributed. Poverty exists in overcrowded parts of the wealthy cities.

In the mountain villages, peasants live without running water or electricity or streets. The farmers must earn enough money to keep the land they have cleared, or they will lose it to ranchers and plantation owners. Producing illegal drugs earns them enough money to keep their land.

The Cartels

The big money from cocaine production in Colombia is made by the drug lords of

24 the cartels. The cartels distribute the cocaine through powerful networks of smugglers and distributors.

Political struggles have long existed in Colombia between the "haves" and the "have-nots." Violence and killing have been common. The cartel leaders have been responsible in many cases. They have kidnaped and murdered politicians and judges who have opposed them. The Colombian government is fighting back against the cartels and their corruption. In recent years the strength of the Medellín cartel has been broken and its leaders have been jailed. But other groups such as the Cali cartel have sprung up to carry on the drug work. And so the struggles in Colombia continue.

Bolivia

The Andes Mountains make up about one third of Bolivia. The mountain people are isolated from each other and from trade. Economic growth has been slow. As in Colombia, there is a mixture of wealth and poverty in Bolivian cities, and much unemployment.

In the mountains, the peasants have found that they can earn more from coca leaves than any other crop they raise. The processing plants of Colombia and the trafficking networks of the cartels are nearby.

Terrorism

Reformers in the Bolivian government have tried to remedy the problems of poverty. They have tried to replace coca farming with other crops. But political unrest occupies the government. Terrorist groups plot to overthrow the government. One of their violent techniques is the use of bombs. In 1988 an attack was made on the visiting U.S. Secretary of State George Shultz. U.S. missionaries were killed in 1989, and a U.S. Marine guard-house was attacked in 1990. Combatting these guerrilla groups takes money and resources that the Bolivian government lacks.

Peru

The Andes Mountains also run through Peru. They create isolation and limit growth of the economy. Peru also has a division between the wealthy and the poor. Large cities have shantytowns with squalid conditions. Reforms have been attempted, but Peru has never achieved economic stability.

It is believed that guerrilla groups like *Sendero Luminoso*, Shining Path, support themselves with money from the drug trade.

Like their neighbors in Colombia and Bolivia, the poor of Peru turned to raising coca leaves for cocaine.

The Peruvian government faces violent attack by revolutionaries. A strong guerrilla group is known as the Shining Path, or in Spanish, *Sendero Luminoso.* The Shining Path has been responsible for killing peasants, government workers, police, and religious workers. Through brutality, threats, and murder, the Shining Path intimidates the people of the countryside. It is believed that the group supports itself with money gained from the drug trade.

Myanmar

Burma is one of the "Golden Triangle" countries in Southeast Asia. In 1989 it changed its name to Myanmar. It is the main source of heroin to the world.

At one time Burma was the world's largest exporter of rice. But civil war, foreign invasion, and political strife have all but destroyed the economy. The standard of living of the people dropped to a low level. When the Chinese invaded the country in 1949, they brought with them the opium poppy. It turned out to be a

28 product that the poor peasants could export to the world.

Myanmar has faced years of turmoil and struggle. Because of the poor economy, the government cannot do enough to improve living conditions. This has led to uprisings, rebellions, and military takeovers. Thousands of people have died in these upheavals. Many factions form in the villages. It is said that some of these groups are funded by illegal opium money.

Thailand

Thailand is also part of the Golden Triangle. Compared to other countries of Asia, the economy of Thailand is good. Most Thais are farmers, producing rice for their own use and for export. Medical care and education have improved. Cities like Bangkok, the capital, are modern. In the countryside, however, where most of the people live, the standard of living is lower. The small villages have inadequate medical and educational services. Some Thais have turned to producing the heroin poppy and the drugs it produces.

In the last 60 years Thailand has suffered under 25 violent overthrows of the government.

Laos

Bordering Thailand on the northeast, Laos is the third country of the Golden Triangle. It is one of the poorest countries in the world. Health conditions are very bad. About 90 percent of the people are farmers, but they cannot trade their produce because of lack of transportation.

Besides difficult economic problems, the people have seen frequent civil war and have been invaded and ruled by other countries. As in other drug-producing countries, the poor can be less poor by growing, processing, and selling illegal drugs. It has been reported that Laos has used profits from the heroin traffic to help make ends meet.

Recently the Lao government has been developing a plan to work with U.S. agents to reduce drug production in its country.

As long as they are in need, the poor of the drug-producing countries will turn to illegal crops to avoid starvation. As long as there is political unrest, the drug lords will have power to influence policy. Many problems must be addressed to put a stop to production of these deadly narcotics.

CHAPTER 4

Drug Crimes and Punishments Worldwide

*T*he United States provides mandatory jail sentences for drug crimes. Over half of current federal prisoners are serving time for drug-related crimes. To date, no one has received the death penalty for drug trafficking. It is quite a different story in other countries. Two Asian countries, Malaysia and Singapore, have very severe penalties for drug possession and trafficking. The laws apply to visitors as well as citizens.

In both Malaysia and Singapore the legal systems are very strict. Those convicted of crimes suffer the prescribed penalty. Unlike the judicial system of the United States, no plea bargaining is possible, and there is no chance of appeal once a verdict is reached.

Death for Dealing

In the Malaysian airport hangs a sign reading, "Death to Da Da." Da da is the Malaysian word for drugs. In less than 20 years about 250 people, both Malaysians and foreign visitors, have been sentenced to death for breaking the drug laws. In 1986 two Australian men were hanged under the strict Malaysian antidrug laws. Brian Geoffrey Chambers and Kevin Barlow were found guilty of possession of heroin. There had been many appeals for clemency from relatives of the men as well as Amnesty International and the Australian and British governments. Then Prime Minister Margaret Thatcher of Great Britain and the Australian Prime Minister, Bob Hawke, made personal attempts to intervene on behalf of Chambers and Barlow, to no avail.

In 1990 a Malaysian mother of five was hanged for possession of marijuana. Malaysian law does not discriminate on the basis of race, sex, or nationality. The possession of drugs results in prosecution, and sentences are strictly applied.

Like Malaysia, Singapore applies a

32 | death-by-hanging penalty for drug offenses. Visitors who are convicted should be aware that no intervention from their own government can help them.

Thailand also punishes drug traffickers swiftly and violently. Those convicted of drug smuggling face death by hanging.

Some visitors to these countries have not believed that death sentences would be executed. *They are.* Nationality has no bearing on the punishment for a crime. Even the Queen of England was unable to save one of her subjects from hanging.

A Different Code of Law

South America does not inflict the death penalty for drug trafficking. But that does not mean that persons convicted of drug crimes have an easy time. Under U.S. law, a person arrested is considered innocent until proven guilty. South American countries operate under the Napoleonic Code. Under this code, a person arrested is considered guilty until proven innocent.

The South American judicial system is more complicated than that in the U.S. The system of courts and judges is very complex, and the process takes a long time. A prisoner can await trial for many years—and he or she waits in jail.

The penalty for using or dealing illegal drugs is death
in some countries, as shown by this warning sign in
a Malaysian airport.

34   People convicted of drug crimes in South American countries face long jail sentences. The conditions of many of the prisons are very bad, and the treatment is very harsh.

Considering the death penalty and the harsh prison conditions in many countries, it would seem that drug trafficking would stop. In some countries, change has indeed occurred. The book and movie "The Midnight Express" tell the story of an American, Billy Hayes, confined in a Turkish jail for breaking the drug laws.

For smuggling four pounds of hashish, a form of marijuana, he was sentenced to life in prison, but his sentence was reduced to 30 years. Along with Turkish prisoners, he lived in filth and was beaten and tortured.

Turkey also has enacted social reform programs. As a result, the country has been able to control drug trafficking within its borders.

The Trade Goes On

In many Asian countries, however, in spite of harsh laws and punishments, drug trafficking continues. Smuggling of heroin is a lucrative business, yielding enormous profits. Greed encourages the traffickers

Manuel Noriega, former head of the Defense Force in Panama, is serving a forty-year sentence in the United States for his role in drug trafficking.

36 to risk their lives for the drug trade.

In South American countries where the drug laws are strict and punishments severe, the drugs lords rarely are the ones to be convicted. Those who control the trafficking are wealthy and powerful. They are able to bribe officials or surround themselves with small armies of guards.

Extradition

In efforts to change this situation, the United States has moved to sign treaties of extradition with some South American countries. Extradition is the moving of a suspected criminal from one country to another to stand trial. With such a treaty in place, if a drug lord in Colombia were indicted by a U.S. court for trafficking in drugs in the United States, the suspect would be sent to the United States to stand trial. If convicted, the criminal would serve a sentence in a U.S. jail.

One foreign drug lord who stood trial in the U.S. is Manuel Antonio Noriega. General Noriega was a powerful figure in Panama. For years he had cooperated with the U.S. government, and he was considered a friend. Over time, however, it became clear that the General was heavily involved in drug trafficking. He

In the United States, officers of the Drug Enforcement Agency (DEA) work to combat drug production and trade.

was indicted in a Florida court. President Eric Delvalle of Panama asked Noriega to step down as head of the Defense Force. General Noriega refused to step down or to accept extradition. Instead he seized power in Panama and declared war on the U.S. In a military action called Operation Just Cause, the U.S. invaded Panama and took Noriega prisoner. Noriega stood trial in Florida, was found guilty of drug trafficking, and was sentenced to 40 years in a U.S. prison.

Extradition treaties are not popular with the drug lords. They would rather keep control of their fate through their influence and power.

37

CHAPTER 5

Stopping Drug Trafficking

*D*rug trafficking is a major problem. It is controlled by many large, powerful networks. These world networks may be called cartels, syndicates, or mafia. Whatever the name, the violence and corruption remain the same.

According to federal drug agents, it would be as impossible to stop the drug traffic as to stop all crime. As long as there is demand for drugs, there will be drug traffickers.

The work of the drug law-enforcement agents is to manage the problem and try to reduce the trafficking and the crime *38* and violence that go with it.

The DEA

To confront the problem, the U.S. government has designated the Drug Enforcement Administration (DEA) to be the lead agency. The DEA is part of the Department of Justice.

Agents of the DEA work both in the U.S. and in foreign countries. In other countries the agents work with local law officers as advisers in combatting drug production and trade. They also gather information about the networks moving the drugs to the U.S.

There is great risk in the work done by DEA agents and others in fighting drug trafficking. Drug network leaders surround themselves with heavily armed security forces.

The Customs Service

Other federal agencies are also involved in this work. The U.S. Customs Service and the Coast Guard patrol the borders to stop illegal smuggling. Besides boats, drugs are also brought in by plane, by car, and even on foot. Customs agents have thousands of miles of borders to monitor.

DEA agents seek information in other countries on points of entry for illegal

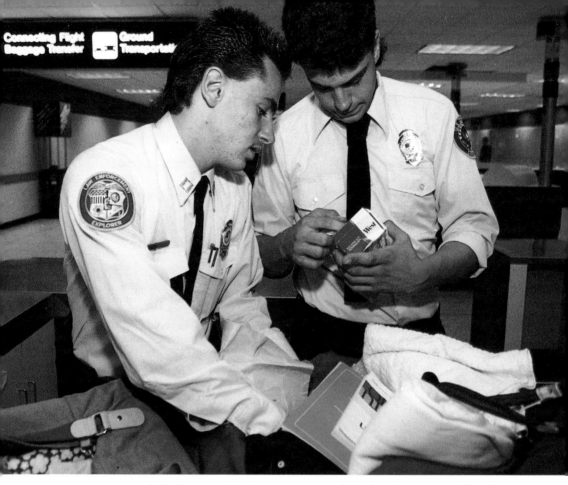

U.S. Customs Service agents patrol the borders to stop illegal smuggling of drugs.

drugs. Stopping drugs at the border is called interdiction. Because of the vast number of people involved in smuggling and the many available points of entry into the U.S., interdiction is extremely difficult.

The FBI
The Federal Bureau of Investigation (FBI) is also involved in the drug trafficking offensive. Agents coordinate

information with the DEA and with other law-enforcement officials.

The IRS

The Internal Revenue Service (IRS) is also working on the trafficking problem. The IRS oversees payment of taxes on money earned in the U.S. Traffickers earn large amounts of illegal money on which no taxes are paid. The IRS traces the illegal earnings and prosecutes the criminals. IRS agents also coordinate their work with the other drug agencies involved.

The ATF

The Bureau of Alcohol, Tobacco and Firearms (ATF) fights the federal crimes associated with drug trafficking. Illegal firearms are responsible for much of the drug-related violence, so the ATF agents frequently work on the dangerous front of the drug war.

Besides the federal agencies working on this problem, many state and local law-enforcement agencies are at work.

State and Local Efforts

In each State Police Department, officers are assigned to drug investigation cases.

Law-enforcement officers of every level can find themselves
investigating a drug crime.

But they are not the only officers working on the problem. Many of the crimes committed are related to illegal drugs. Any police officer may find himself or herself investigating a call that turns out to be a drug crime.

Law-enforcement officers of city and county police departments are called on to investigate drug crimes as well. They too must be trained and outfitted to react to the violence and crime involving illegal drugs. They may gain information in their investigations that can link drug activity to other areas nationally or in foreign countries.

All the agents fighting drug trafficking and crimes associated with it must be able to communicate with each other and coordinate information. This effort requires vast communication networks and many people to relay information.

Foreign Programs

Many other countries of the world have drug enforcement agents at work. In drug-producing countries these agents find and destroy laboratories where the drugs are produced. There have also been attempts to destroy fields where the drug crops are raised.

44   Programs have been set up to teach the farmers to raise other crops to replace the coca leaves or marijuana or opium poppies. These programs have not been widely successful because no other crop earns as much money for the farmers. The crop substitution programs have other problems. When the farmers switch to a new crop, they may not be able to sell it. In some countries the road systems and transportation are so poor that legal crops cannot reach a market. The drug networks assure the farmers of a good price for the crop as well as adequate transportation systems.

Around the globe, law-enforcement agents are fighting the drug traffic. But law enforcement is only one means of stemming the flow of illegal drugs. DEA agents stress that reducing the demand is another important means of reducing the traffic and the violence associated with it. Demand for drugs can be reduced through education and treatment. There is a need, they say, for a strong policy of continuing education on drug abuse. There is also great need for more treatment programs for those who want to break their drug addiction.

CHAPTER 6

The Costs of the Drug War

For the nations of the world engaged in battling the drug problem, the war is very costly. The U.S. federal government currently has an annual budget of $12 billion to fight illegal drugs. The funds are spent on federal programs and for assistance to state programs.

We have looked at some of the many federal agencies working to control the drug traffic. Thousands of people are employed in the fight by the federal government. This requires salaries, offices, and equipment.

When federal agents travel from state to state or abroad on business, transportation costs must be paid. Agents working

46 | in foreign countries must also have places
to work and live.

State and local law-enforcement agencies have drug-related expenses, too.
Violence against people and property has
increased sharply. More police and more
training, protection, and equipment are
required.

Prisons Are Expensive

Drug-related crime puts a financial strain
on the legal system as well. Defendants
arrested for drug crimes must have a trial,
which involves great expense.

Once convicted of a drug crime, the
criminal is sent to prison, where it costs
thousands of dollars a month to support
each inmate. As prisons and jails become
crowded, new ones must be built, at costs
running into the millions of dollars.

Treatment Centers Are Scarce

People with addictions require treatment.
Not enough treatment centers are available for the people who want to get off
drugs. Most have waiting lists.

It would cost hundreds of millions of
dollars to build the necessary number of
treatment centers in the U.S.

Treatment and rehabilitation are not

the only medical expenses related to drug abuse. Many people are injured as a result of violent drug crimes. Some are the victims of dealers battling over turf. Some are victims of addicts desperate for money. Some are family members of drug abusers.

Other victims of drug abuse are babies born to addicted mothers. The babies suffer from the same addiction as the mother. The care of crack babies has been estimated to be in the hundreds of millions of dollars.

AIDS is another medical problem requiring intensive treatment. AIDS is not caused by drug abuse, but the HIV virus is spread by people sharing needles to inject drugs.

The Need for Education
Education is an important defense in the drug war. Developing and expanding education programs is expensive. The programs must be made available all over the country. Different programs must be developed that are geared to people of various ages.

Foreign Efforts to Fight the War
The expenses mentioned so far have been those of the United States. Many other countries are facing the same high cost of

48 | fighting the drug war. The burden is a
further strain on already frail economies.

But many of the poor nations have
joined in the efforts to stop the drug
traffic. They have implemented social
programs to replace illegal crops with
legal crops. Every dollar spent on a drug
problem is a dollar that cannot be spent
on needed health, food, and educational
programs.

The final and greatest cost of the drug
war is the cost in human life.

Thousands of people have been killed
as a result of illegal drugs. In 1989 in
Colombia, presidential candidate Luis
Carlos Galán was murdered as a result of
his plans for criminal reform. In the fol-
lowing year, two other Colombian presidential candidates were killed for their
strong reform measures.

Also killed are drug enforcement
agents. Hundreds are killed each year
worldwide. In Mexico, in 1985, a DEA
agent named Enrique Camerena was
kidnaped, tortured, and murdered.

The cost of the drug war is enormous.
Money and lives are being lost to the
battle. The problems caused by illegal
drugs are draining the resources of many
nations.

Education is one of the most effective defenses in the war against drugs.

CHAPTER 7

The Question of Legalization

*T*he drug war seems to many observers to be endless and unwinnable. Some frustrated citizens and politicians in the United States have looked to a different solution. They have suggested legalization of drugs.

Those who favor legalization believe it would stop the trafficking in drugs by reducing the profits. If drugs could be obtained through legal sources, they say, the power of the drug lords would be lessened. This, in turn, would end the violence and the expense of law-enforcement activities.

Those who argue against the legalization of drugs point out that it would not

effectively stop the smuggling and the
black market. It would not make highly
addictive drugs available to those who
were under age or for some other reason
could not obtain legal drugs. These people would become the targets of illegal
drug pushers.

Failed Experiments

As examples of the failure of legalized or
decriminalized drug practices, opponents
cite England and the Netherlands.

In England a heroin addict can legally
obtain the drug from a physician. But still
the number of addicts and drug abusers
continues to grow. The black market and
drug smuggling continue to flourish. In
1992, European officials met in London
to coordinate their efforts in fighting drug
use among the young. Drug trafficking in
England and Europe is on the rise.

Relaxation of drug laws in the Netherlands did not stop illegal drug trafficking.
The black market and the crimes related
to it continued, and the violence grew. In
Rotterdam a minister was allowed to
open his church as a free zone for drug
use. He maintained that the addicts were
sick people in need of care. After two
years he had to close the church. It was

52 overrun by gangsters dealing illegal drugs to the addicts. His experiment had failed.

The proponents of drug legalization say that money currently spent to fight the war on drugs could be used to administer rehabilitation programs. This would eventually reduce the amount of taxpayer money spent on fighting drugs.

Those opposed to legalization disagree. They say there is no evidence that the rate of drug addiction would decrease. Rather, they predict that it would increase dramatically. There would then be enormous amounts of money spent on rehabilitation. Others point to the current cost of medical care for drug-addicted babies. This cost is passed on to the government. And opponents say it would only increase.

Other difficult questions would be involved in legalization of drugs. How would such a program be handled? What drugs would be legalized? Who would make the decision? Where would drugs be made available? Who could get the legal drugs? There is little agreement on these issues among proponents of legalization.

CHAPTER 8

Getting Involved in Drug Prevention

*T*he drug problem is large. It is complex. It seems so overwhelming that there is nothing one person can do to help. But each person *can* become involved in putting an end to the drug problem. Yes, even a teenager still in high school can become proactive.

Becoming proactive means getting involved with a problem and working toward a solution. A teen can become proactive in drug prevention in three ways: education, legislation, and registration.

Education

You may not realize it, but you have just taken a step in proactive drug prevention.

53

Many schools offer programs that teach students about the dangers of drug abuse.

By reading this book you have further educated yourself about the problem. You have learned about some of the political issues involved. You have become more aware of the scope of the problem.

There are many areas in which to continue your personal education. Health issues related to drugs do not belong just to the drug user. We know that AIDS is spread by intravenous drug use. We know that drug addiction is passed on to the babies of addicted mothers. There are also other related issues to learn about.

54   Every community has law-enforcement

problems and economic problems related
to drugs. When you take the time to learn
about any of these issues, you are becoming more proactive.

Learn About the Problem

Libraries offer information. Besides books
and magazines, libraries often have free
pamphlets of information about drugs.

Many agencies and groups are dedi-
cated to drug abuse prevention. They
may offer literature, films, speakers,
counseling, or treatment. A handy refer-
ence is the phone book. County, city,
state, and federal government agencies
are grouped together on blue pages in
most phone directories. Drug-related
services can be listed in several ways.
First look under "D" for drugs. Also
check under "A" for alcohol. Many
agencies combine alcohol and drug
services in one office.

A second source is the yellow pages.
Under "D" for drug abuse you may find
listings of organizations and agencies
that offer help and education for drug
prevention.

Find out if your school has a drug-
awareness or prevention program. If it
does, get involved. If not, ask a teacher

56 or administrator. You may be able to help in starting a program.

Legislation

Legislation is the process of making laws. Yes, you can be involved in this process. It is as easy as writing a letter. As you become more aware of drug issues, you will hear about proposed laws, budget cuts, and other actions that politicians are taking. You have a right to let them know your opinion on what they are doing or not doing. For example, you may hear that the governor is asking for a law that every school must have a drug-prevention program. If you think it is a good idea, you can write to your state legislator and give your opinion.

To get the names and addresses of your state legislator and your U.S. Senator and Representative, you can use the phone book again. In the blue government listing pages for your city or county, find "Election Board" or "Elections Supervisor." This office should be able to give you the names and addresses you want. Your letters can make a difference.

If you are part of a drug education program in your school or community center, you can suggest to others that they become more proactive by writing to politicians about drug-related issues.

Try a Petition

Another effective way to influence legislation is through a petition. A petition is a letter of request signed by a group of people and sent to a public official.

A high school student read in the paper that the state legislature was discussing closing a drug treatment center in her community. She had also read that treatment programs in the area were so few that many people were being turned away. The student discussed the problem with other members of her drug-awareness program. They all agreed that something should be done to keep the center open. The proactive student suggested sending a petition to the legislators. The group wrote the petition letter and began collecting signatures. School officials permitted them to solicit signatures in front of the school. Next they got approval from a grocery store manager to set up a table in front of the store and inform shoppers about the issue and ask them to sign. When the petition was long enough to be impressive, the students

58 | sent it to the state legislators. They had made their opinion known.

Through the petition process you can be proactive in two ways. First, you educate others about a problem and a method of working for a solution. Second, you get involved in affecting legislation.

Registration

Another proactive step you can take in drug abuse prevention is registering to vote. If you are not yet old enough to vote, you should still be aware of how to do it. In most areas a person need only go to the nearest post office or public library to pick up a voter registration form. In 1993, President Bill Clinton signed the "Motor Voter Bill." This new law enables people to register to vote at the Department of Motor Vehicles and many other public offices.

Through the voting process, citizens can show approval or disapproval of the public policies. Before voting, you must inform yourself of the issues. In that way you will be able to cast your vote for the officials who are tackling the problems most important to you.

As you become more proactive in drug

abuse prevention, you will also become aware of which officials and legislators are responding to the problem. If you are not old enough to vote, you can still exert influence by discussing your concerns and your opinions with teachers, parents, relatives, and older friends. You can encourage them to get involved and to vote.

Being proactive in drug abuse prevention can be as simple as reading newspapers, sharing information with friends, and walking into a voting booth. It can also be a more elaborate program of involvement.

Drug abuse is eroding the quality of life of people around the world. It is depleting the human and financial resources that could be better used addressing other world issues. If we are to meet the global needs for food, shelter, medical care, and education, everyone needs to get involved and work together to end the drug abuse epidemic.

Glossary
Explaining New Words

black market   The illegal buying and selling of goods.

cartel   International organization that regulates the production and price of a product.

coca plant   Plant from which cocaine is produced.

cocaine   Strong stimulant drug made from the leaves of the coca plant.

cocaine base   The pure form of cocaine that is mixed with other substances to reduce its strength and increase the amount available for sale.

cocaine HLC   Cocaine hydrochloride, a very strong form of cocaine.

coup   The sudden and violent overthrow of a government.

drug trafficking   The smuggling, transporting, and selling of illegal drugs.

economics   Method of sharing goods, services, and wealth.

export To ship something to another country for sale.

extradition The surrender of an alleged criminal to another country or state for trial.

Golden Triangle Name given to the areas of Myanmar, Thailand, and Laos where opium poppies are grown for the production of heroin.

heroin Drug manufactured from opium poppies.

interdiction The act of stopping or impeding.

mafia An organization of criminals.

marijuana plant Plant whose leaves are used to produce the illegal drug marijuana.

morphine Drug made from the opium poppy and used medically as a painkiller.

opium Drug produced from the opium poppy and used to make heroin or morphine.

politics Methods used by officials to run a government.

syndicate Group of people working together on a project that requires large amounts of money.

For Further Reading

Beckett, Ian. *Conflict in the 20th Century: Southeast Asia from 1945*. New York: Franklin Watts, 1986.

Blair, David N. *Bolivia*. New York: Harper & Row, Publishers, Inc., 1990.

Hawkes, Nigel. *The Heroin Trail*. New York: Gloucester Press, 1986.

Hyde, Margaret O. *Drug Wars*. New York: Franklin Watts, 1990.

Johnson, Joan. *America's War on Drugs*. New York: Franklin Watts, 1990.

Parker, Steve. *The Drug War*. New York: Gloucester Press, 1990.

Pearce, Jenny. *Colombia, The Drug War*. New York: Gloucester Press, 1990.

Index

Acknowledgments

Special thanks to Craig N. Chretien, Assistant Special Agent in Charge, Baltimore District Office, Drug Enforcement Administration; and Frank S. Franco, Special Agent, Drug Enforcement Administration, for their assistance in providing information for this book.

About the Author

Peggy Santamaria is a graduate of the University of Maryland. Since 1977, she has worked in community banks as a customer service representative and a loan officer.

Before starting her banking career, she was a contributing writer and photographer for a local newpaper. She has also taught both the elementary and middle school levels.

As a volunteer, Ms. Santamaria has worked on behalf of the mentally disabled in a theater arts program and as a fund raiser. She lives in Baltimore County with her husband, Ed, their daughters, Aimee, Anne, and Christina, and an assortment of pets.

Photo Credits

Cover photo: by Maje Waldo; pp. 22, 26, 33, 35, 37, 40, 42: © AP/Wide World Photo; all other photos by Lauren Piperno.